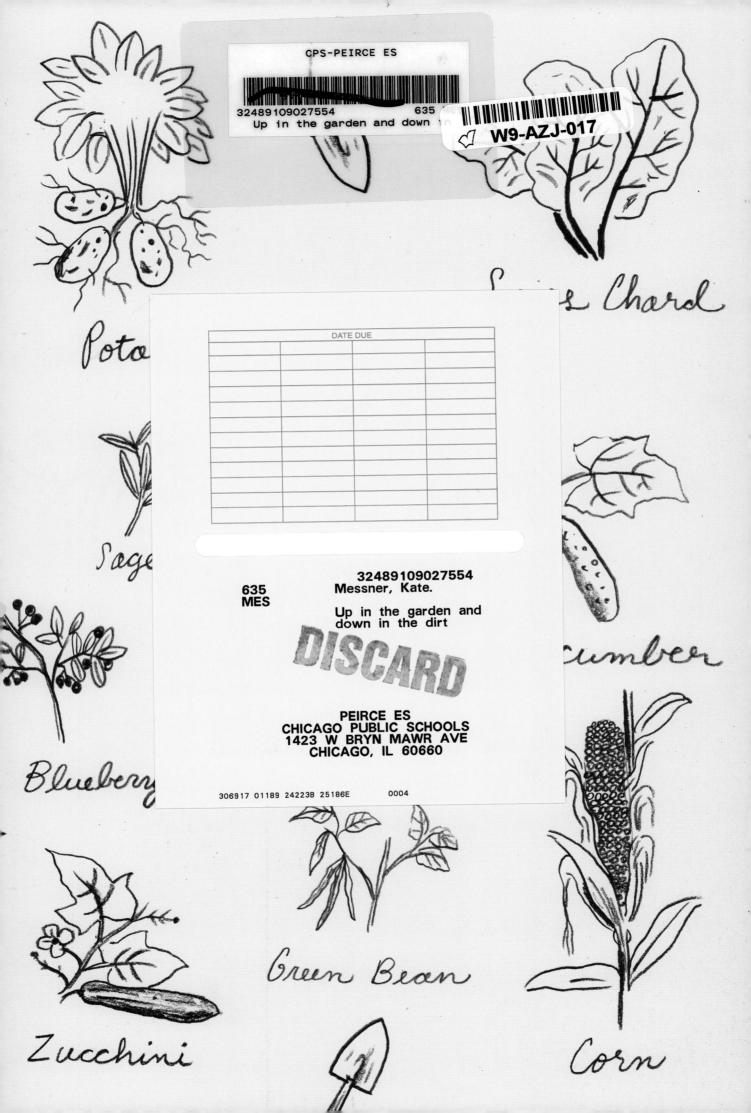

Potato

Swiss Chard

Sage

Cucumber

Blueberry

Zucchini

Green Bean

Corn

For the Burns family of gardeners—Loree, Gerry, Cat,
Ben, and Sam —K. M.

For my lifelong garden companion, Jennifer —C. S. N.

Library of Congress Cataloging-in-Publication Data:
Messner, Kate, author.
Up in the garden and down in the dirt /
by Kate Messner ; with art by Christopher Silas Neal.
pages cm
Summary: "Up in the garden, the world is full of green—leaves and sprouts,
growing vegetables, ripening fruit. But down in the dirt there is a busy world
of earthworms digging, snakes hunting, skunks burrowing, and all the other
animals that make a garden their home. In this exuberant book, discover
the wonder and activity that lie hidden between the stalks, under the shade
of leaves . . . and down in the dirt."— Provided by publisher.
Audience: Ages 4-8.
Audience: K to grade 3.
ISBN 978-1-4521-1936-6 (alk. paper)
1. Gardening—Juvenile literature. 2. Gardens—Juvenile literature.
3. Soils—Composition—Juvenile literature. I. Neal, Christopher Silas,
illustrator. II. Title.
SB457.M47 2015
635—dc23
2014001786

Manufactured in China.

Book design by Amelia May Mack.
Typeset in Jannon Antiqua.
The illustrations in this book were rendered in mixed media.

10 9 8 7 6 5 4 3 2

Chronicle Books LLC
680 Second Street, San Francisco, California 94107

www.chroniclekids.com

Up
in the Garden and
Down
in the Dirt

by Kate Messner with art by Christopher Silas Neal

chronicle books · san francisco

Up in the garden, I stand and plan—
my hands full of seeds and my head full of dreams.

Spring sun shines down to melt the sleepy snow.

Wind whistles through last year's plants, and mud sucks at my rain boots.

"It's not quite time," Nana says. "Down in the dirt, things need to dry out and warm up."

"What's down there?" I ask.

"Down in the dirt is a whole busy world of earthworms and insects, digging and building and stirring up soil. They're already working down in the dirt."

Up in the garden, we snap brittle stalks, scoop rustly armfuls, and wheel away weeds for the chickens. While they squabble and scratch, we spread compost over the soil.

Down in the dirt, pill bugs chew through last year's leaves. I give a gentle poke. They roll up tight and hide in plated suits of armor, roly-poly round.

Up in the garden, it's time to plant. I trail a furrow
with my finger and sprinkle seeds in a careful row.

"Give them a drink," Nana says. We pat them
down to snuggle in the dark.

Down in the dirt, a tomato hornworm rests,
waiting for wings—and the leaves where
she'll lay her eggs.

Up in the garden, carrot plants sprout. Pea blossoms bloom. Wasps are on the prowl, and honeybees visit, legs loaded with pollen.

I weed and wilt in sun so strong even
Nana looks for shade.

Down in the dirt earthworms tunnel deep.
I'm jealous of their cool, damp, dark.

Up in the garden—"Rain shower!"

Nana turns the hose on me!

"Eeeee!"

I hide behind the cucumber vines, but their leaves can't save me. I shiver and laugh, drenched in Nana's rain.

Down in the dirt, water soaks deep. Roots drink it in, and a long-legged spider stilt-walks over the streams.

Up in the garden, there's so much
to eat! Ladybugs feast on aphids.

Nana crunches green beans. I bite a ripe
tomato, warm from the sun. Juice dribbles
down my chin.

Down in the dirt, a robin's beak finds a cricket, a beetle, a grub. Slugs are scrumptious, too.

Up in the garden, we pick cukes and zucchini, harvesting into the dark. Bats swoop through the sunflowers, and I pluck June bugs from the basil until it's time for bed.

Down in the dirt, skunks work the night shift.
They snuffle and dig, and gobble cutworms
while I sleep.

Up in the garden, a praying mantis wakes to
hunt mosquitoes. Nana sprays away the aphids,
and I'm after grasshoppers.

Ready to *swoosh*, but . . .

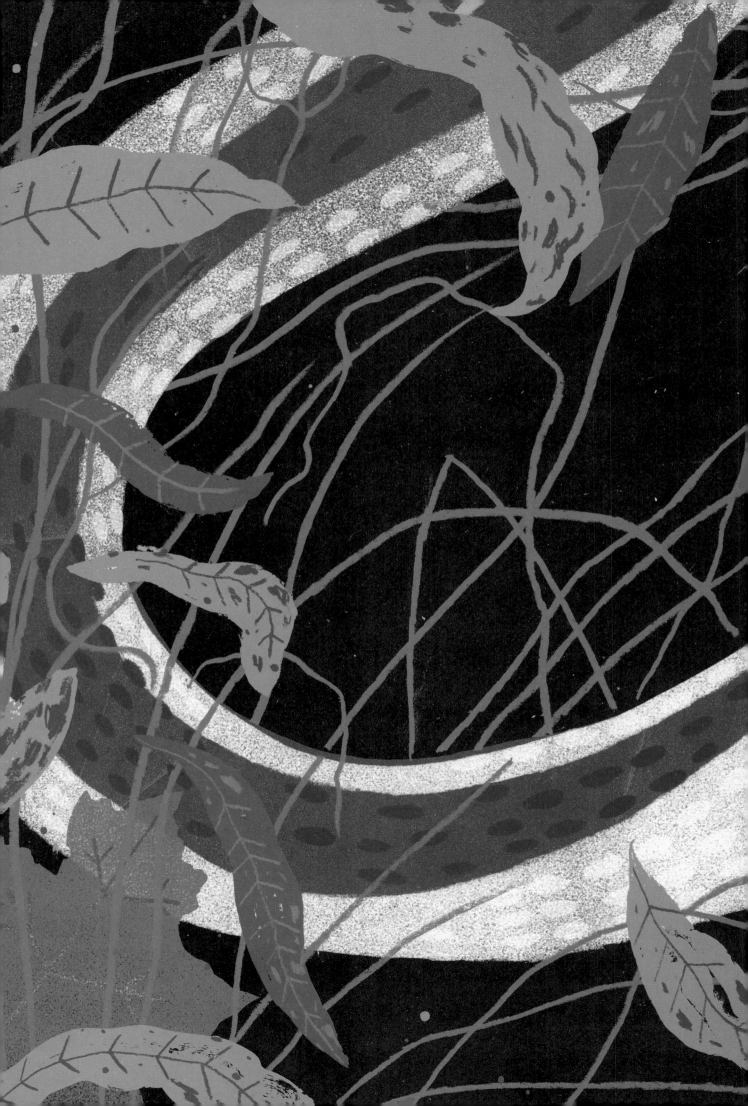

Snap! Someone else is faster!

Down in the dirt, a smooth, shining garter snake crunches on supper.

Up in the garden, the wind grows cool.
Pumpkins blush orange, and sunflowers bow
to September. Nana ties them together to
build a house for reading.

Down in the dirt, an orb weaver spins her web, strand by silken strand. She'll munch on moths tonight.

Up in the garden, colored leaves litter the squash vines, and we know the cold is coming.

Hurry, hurry, and harvest!

There's enough for the neighbors, too!

Down in the dirt, frantic ants gather what we leave behind. They're storing food for cooler days ahead.

Up in the garden, frost draws lace on leftover leaves, where secret egg sacs hang, waiting for the warm to return. We say good-bye and spread the winter blankets.

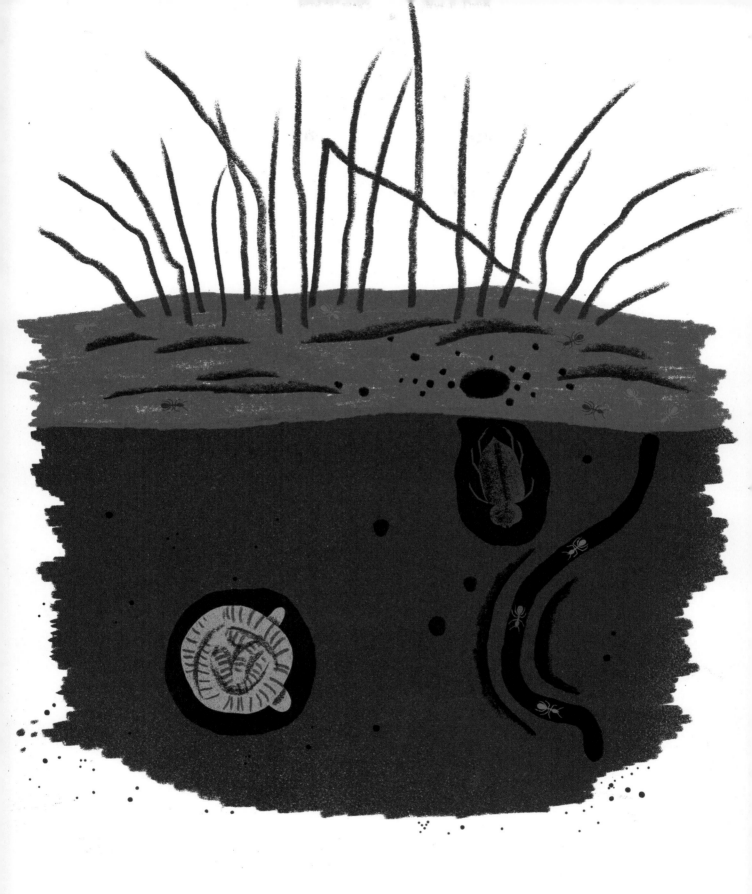

Down in the dirt, beetles burrow. Ants scurry
home. Earthworms curl tight in the dark.

When Grandpa calls us in for soup, an autumn moon is rising.

Up in the garden, dry cornstalks tremble, and the wind smells like winter.

But the long ripe days of summer still rest in the garden beds.

The ladybugs and bumblebees, earthworms and ants are hunkered down, hiding . . . biding their time . . .

dreaming of sunshine and blossoms and sprouts.

Under the bare arms of trees and the blanketing snow,

a whole new garden sleeps

down in the dirt.

Author's Note

Every garden is a community garden. Do you know why? You may work hard planting seeds and pulling weeds, but plants can't thrive without the help of all those smaller gardeners down in the dirt.

Some help by controlling pests that would like to gobble up your broccoli and tomatoes before you have a chance to eat them yourself. Some help by creating tunnels, which bring air into the soil and let water drain more easily. And believe it or not, some help just by going to the bathroom right there next to the green beans. This adds important nutrients to the soil.

A healthy organic garden isn't a garden without bugs—it's packed with lots and lots of living things, all working together with the human gardeners to nurture healthy plants.

Further Reading

A Seed Is Sleepy, by Dianna Hutts Aston, Chronicle Books, 2007

Citizen Scientists: Be a Part of Scientific Discovery from Your Own Backyard, by Loree Griffin Burns, Henry Holt, 2012

Compost Stew: An A to Z Recipe for the Earth, by Mary McKenna Siddals, Tricycle Press, 2010

In the Garden: Who's Been Here?, by Lindsay Barrett George, Greenwillow Books, 2006

Sunflower House, by Eve Bunting, Harcourt Children's Books, 1996

This Year's Garden, by Cynthia Rylant, Atheneum Books for Young Readers, 1986

About the Animals

The animals you met in this book really do live, eat, and work in many vegetable gardens. Some are helpful. Others . . . not so much!

You might think of **chickens** as farm animals, but more and more families are keeping them at home. These backyard pets do double duty, laying eggs for their owners and eating bugs, kitchen scraps, and weeds. Chicken manure makes excellent compost.

Pill bugs aren't really insects at all but terrestrial, or land-based, crustaceans. Their scientific name is *Armadillidium vulgare*, but most people call them pill bugs or roly-poly bugs, nicknames that come from the creature's habit of rolling up into a ball when it feels threatened. Pill bugs eat decaying plants, which helps to add important nutrients to the soil.

The **tomato hornworm** is the colorful larva of an insect called the five-spotted hawk moth, and it's a dreaded garden pest. Adult moths often lay their eggs on tomato leaves, where the larvae emerge to eat. When it's fully grown, a caterpillar burrows into the soil to pupate, and an adult moth emerges about two weeks later to start the process over again.

Honeybees and bumblebees help to pollinate plants in a garden. When they fly from flower to flower, collecting nectar and pollen, they also transfer pollen from one flower to another, leading to fertilization. Without an exchange of pollen, the blossoms on plants like cucumbers, squash, and watermelon would never develop into the fruits and vegetables we eat.

Earthworms are garden heroes! Their tunnels bring air into the soil and make it easier for water to drain. Too much water is bad for plants because it can lead to mold and mildew and prevent roots from getting the oxygen they need. As earthworms burrow, they ingest soil and eat the decomposing roots and leaves. When the dirt comes out of the other end of the worm, as castings, it is finer and softer dirt, full of nutrients to help plants grow.

Long-legged spiders that we see in gardens are often Opiliones, or harvestmen, which are related to true spiders but differ in that they don't have two distinct body sections. Harvestmen don't have venom or silk glands either. They eat decomposing plants as well as some pesky garden insects like aphids and mites.

The **robin**, or *Turdus migratorius*, is just one of many species of birds that might come to the garden to snack on bugs. This is helpful because crickets, beetles, grubs, and slugs can all damage plants. Some gardeners go out of their way to attract insect-eating birds by providing them with small shrubs for cover and bird baths for drinking and bathing.

Bats are also good friends to gardeners. Like birds, they eat many insects that damage plants as well as the mosquitoes that pester you while you're trying to pull weeds at dusk. A single brown bat can devour thousands of insects in a single night.

June bugs, or *Phyllophaga*, are so named because they're common in the months of May and June. The June bug is actually a double threat to gardens: the larval grubs can damage the roots of plants, while the adults devour leaves. Predators like toads and frogs help keep June bugs under control.

Like bats, **skunks** are nighttime predators that gobble garden pests after dark. Skunks love grubs and slugs. However, they have smelly reputations and sometimes dig holes while they're searching for insects, so not all gardeners welcome them.

Cutworms aren't really worms; they're moth larvae that hide during the day and feast at night. Cutworms feed on young plants by eating right through the stems, near the base of the soil, cutting the plant down like a tree. Many gardeners dig up cutworms from the soil and remove them by hand. Predators like skunks help, too.

The **praying mantis** is a welcome garden guest because it has an appetite for aphids—notorious little bugs that suck the sap out of plants, weakening or killing them. The praying mantis also eats beetles and grasshoppers as it grows larger. In the fall, the female mantis mates and lays up to four hundred eggs in a tough brown capsule. If it survives the winter, there will be more hungry praying mantises in the spring!

Grasshoppers may be fun to catch with a butterfly net, but they're no friends to garden plants. They chow down on the leaves of most vegetables, but carrots, beans, and lettuce are among their favorites. Many gardeners hand pick grasshoppers from their plants and count on garden predators to take care of the rest.

Garter snakes are not venomous and won't hurt people, but they're great soldiers in the garden grasshopper war. They tend to live under fallen leaves or in wood piles and don't disturb the garden at all.

Many **orb-weaver spiders** build a new web each evening to capture insects that fly around gardens at night. Most of these webs are made of two kinds of silk—sticky capture threads that trap prey and nonsticky threads that the spider uses to get around.

Ants may not be welcome at your harvest picnic, but they can be beneficial in the garden. Ants often crawl from plant to plant looking for nectar, so they can help pollinate plants. Like earthworms, they also help to bring air into the soil with their tunnels so plant roots can grow down more easily.

Marigold

Borage

Crocus

Tulip

Nasturtium

Rhododendron

Aster

Milkweed